CEREMONIES and CELEBRATIONS

Pamela McDowell

Weigl

Published by Weigl Educational Publishers Limited
6325 10th Street SE
Calgary, Alberta T2H 2Z9
Website: www.weigl.ca

Library and Archives Canada Cataloguing in Publication data available upon request.
Fax 403-233-7769 for the attention of the Publishing Records department.

ISBN 978-1-4872-0185-2 (hardcover)
ISBN 978-1-4872-0186-9 (softcover)
ISBN 978-1-4872-0187-6 (multi-user eBook)

Printed in the United States of America in North Mankato, Minnesota
1 2 3 4 5 6 7 8 9 0 18 17 16 15 14

062014
WEP110614

Art Director: Terry Paulhus

Weigl acknowledges Getty Images, Alamy, CP Images, Glenbow Museum, and the Canadian
Museum of History as the primary image suppliers for this title.

Every reasonable effort has been made to trace ownership and to obtain permission to reprint
copyright material. The publishers would be pleased to have any errors or omissions brought
to their attention so that they may be corrected in subsequent printings.

We acknowledge the financial support of the Government of Canada through the Canada
Book Fund for our publishing activities.

Contents

Ceremonies and celebrations are an important part of most societies. Celebrations mark important life events and honour the lives of people when they die. Sometimes, these events become more formal. Rituals, or traditional ways of celebrating, become ceremonies. Special people, music, foods, and places are important parts of a ceremony.

All of Canada's First Nations had celebrations and ceremonies. Often, people from different communities and even different groups came together for a celebration. Powwows are the best-known large celebrations. Powwows featured feasts and competitions in dancing and drumming. Other celebrations focussed on life events, such as marriage or death. Many ceremonies were based on spiritual beliefs.

ALGONQUIN

Sage and sweetgrass

Many Algonquin ceremonies and celebrations were based on spiritual beliefs. Some ceremonies were only performed by **shamans**. The smudge ceremony helped people cleanse themselves or get rid of a negative influence. In the smudge ceremony, the person burned plants and herbs and fanned the smoke toward their body. Sage and **sweetgrass** were often burned in the ceremony. The Algonquin believed sage would remove negative energy and sweetgrass would bring positive energy.

Powwows were an important and well-known Algonquin celebration. The Algonquin word *pauwau* means "gathering." During a powwow, people from many Algonquin groups joined together to enjoy singing, dancing, drumming, and feasting.

Smudge Ceremony

During the smudge ceremony, the Algonquin waved the smoke into their hair. They believed their hair would collect the positive energy from the smudge.

Shamans

Shamans were Algonquin religious leaders. Djasakids were shamans that could consult the spirits about the future.

BLACKFOOT

In search of a vision

The Blackfoot used visions to connect with spirits. These spirits were often part of the natural world, such as the Sun or Moon, or animals, such as the bison, eagle, beaver, or bird. During a ceremony called a vision quest, a young man or young woman travelled a great distance, and then **fasted** and prayed for several days. The spirit that visited the person during the fast became his or her guardian.

The Blackfoot performed some ceremonies before a bison hunt. The hunt could only be successful if the ceremony had been done correctly. This was important because the Blackfoot depended on the bison for survival.

Animal Spirits

The Blackfoot believed that animals had strong spirits and supernatural powers.

Call of the Bison

Songs, prayers, and dances were performed to call in the bison before a hunt.

CREE

Celebrating life

Cree families and communities often came together to mark important events in people's lives. Ceremonies and celebrations honoured family, friends, and nature. They also allowed people to give thanks for their good fortunes.

The Cree celebrated the time when a child learned to walk with a Walking Out Ceremony. The child was dressed in traditional clothes decorated with symbols of animals hunted by the Cree. The family guided the child to a special tent for the ceremony, which was led by a shaman or **elder**. After the ceremony, the child and parents formed a circle around a tree they had decorated.

Walking Out

The Walking Out Ceremony was a special event for a child who was about two years old.

Powwows

The Cree welcomed other First Nations, including the Sioux, Dakota, and Dene, to their powwows.

HAIDA

Importance of potlatch

High-ranking Haida people organized ceremonies and celebrations for the community. The potlatch was the most important gathering. Chiefs were at the centre of this celebration, where people gathered to feast and display their wealth. Guests were seated in the order of their **social status**. Special foods were served in feast dishes, which were artistically carved and painted.

A potlatch was sometimes held after the death of a noble person. During this ceremony, a totem pole was carved and raised. A potlatch could also be held after a cedar-plank house was built. This type of house took great effort to build. The new homeowner would give a potlatch to thank the people who had helped.

Mortuary Pole
A **mortuary** pole was carved to honour someone who died.

HURON

Celebrations for each season

Huron celebrations followed the cycle of the seasons. In the spring, the Huron celebrated the Maple Festival. They danced, feasted, played games, and made maple syrup. The Planting Festival in April or May celebrated the beginning of a new farming year. During this celebration, the Huron feasted and prayed for good growing conditions and crops. In the summer, they celebrated the Strawberry Festival and Green Corn Festival. Celebrations in the fall gave thanks for a good harvest.

In the winter, the Huron celebrated Ononharoia. This was a spiritual ceremony that chased away evil spirits that brought disease and illness. Throughout the year, these celebrations were announced by a person who walked around the village, calling out the details. The older this person was, the more important the celebration was.

Strawberries

The Huron knew it was time to plant beans, pumpkins, and corn when the strawberries began to ripen.

Maple Tree

The Huron celebrated the maple tree in early spring, when the plant began to bud, or bloom.

Iroquois

Offering thanks to the Great Spirit

The Iroquois gathered for many celebrations to give thanks for good harvests and other important events throughout the year. They celebrated the Green Corn Festival in August at the beginning of the corn harvest. People gave speeches of thanks, danced, feasted, and played games for several days. They did it all again during the Harvest Festival, at the end of the corn harvest.

The largest Iroquois celebration was the Midwinter Festival. The people spent six days at the beginning of the new year giving thanks to the Great Spirit. Other celebrations included the Maple Festival, Planting Ceremony, Thunder Ceremony, and Strawberry Festival.

Dried Corn
The Iroquois ate little corn when it was fresh. Most of the crop was harvested and dried for the winter.

MI'KMAQ

Sweating ceremony

An ancient Mi'kmaq cleansing ceremony was held in a sweat lodge. The sweat lodge was made from willow branches shaped in a dome, like a **wigwam**. The fire was in the centre, and the door always faced east. The sweat lodge was a place to pray and purify a person's mind and body. Often, 4 to 12 people took part in the ceremony. Rocks in the fire created heat and steam that caused participants to sweat. Mi'kmaq believed sweating removed impurities from the body. Afterwards, participants were spiritually and physically clean.

Other Mi'kmaq ceremonies thanked the Creator for blessings, health, and food. The Mid-Winter Feast was held after the first new moon of the year. The people celebrated with stories, speeches, dances, and food.

Sweat Lodge
The sweat lodge was a place
of spiritual communication.

OJIBWA

Gathering together

Ojibwa from different villages gathered together for ceremonies and celebrations during the year. During the Feast of the Dead, the people honoured those who had died during the past year. This celebration featured feasting, dancing, games, and contests. Later, the guests would be given gifts by the host village. The Ojibwa came together for powwows, too. These traditional celebrations included competitions for dancers, drummers, and singers.

The Ojibwa celebrated harvests throughout the year. The First Fruits ceremony in late summer celebrated the wild rice harvest. The rice was wrapped in tobacco leaves and placed in water. Then, the Ojibwa burned sweet sage spice. The smoke from this carried their thanks to the Great Spirit.

Great Spirit Offering
The first rice grains the Ojibwa harvested were offered to the Great Spirit.

Powwow
For the Ojibwa, a powwow was both a joyful gathering and a sacred event.

Activity

Create a New Celebration

Many First Nations celebrations marked important events that happened every year. If you could create a new celebration, how would you mark the end of school each year?

Materials: a piece of lined paper divided into four equal squares, pencil

Directions

1. Label the first square Music. Write down the titles of three songs you think celebrate the end of school or the start of summer.

2. Label the second square Feasts. Write down five foods that could be shared with classmates during an end-of-school celebration.

3. Label the third square Competitions. Make a list of four competitions that would test your classmates. Try to think of academic, sports, and musical tests.

4. Label the fourth square Games. Make a list of four games that a large group could play.

On another sheet of paper, draw the same four squares and create a celebration for the start of the school year.

What's Online

To learn more about First Nations ceremonies and celebrations, visit the following websites.

Cree celebrations
www.creeculture.ca/?q=node/65

Ojibwa celebrations
www.anishinaabemdaa.com/ceremonies.htm

Blackfoot vision quest
www.cbc.ca/history/KidsHomeLE.html

Key Words

elder: a respected older person in the community

fasted: went without food or water for a long period of time

mortuary: related to death and burial

shamans: religious leaders, sometimes called medicine men or women

social status: a person's rank in a society or community

sweetgrass: a plant that grows in wet meadows or beside ponds and marshes

wigwam: a hut made of poles and covered with bark or animal skins

Index